T0354995

Physics of My Homemade Stockfish:
A NIGERIAN DELICACY

DEJI BADIRU

PHYSICS OF MY HOMEMADE STOCKFISH:
A NIGERIAN DELICACY

iUniverse books may be ordered through booksellers or by contacting:

iUniverse
1663 Liberty Drive
Bloomington, IN 47403
www.iuniverse.com
844-349-9409

ISBN: 978-1-6632-6814-3 (sc)
ISBN: 978-1-6632-6815-0 (e)

Print information available on the last page.

iUniverse rev. date: 10/21/2024

ABICS Publications
A Division of
AB International Consulting Services

ABICS PUBLICATIONS
Books for Home, Work, & Leisure

Books in the ABICS Publications Book Series:
www.abicspublications.com

Also visit www.ABICS.com

1. **The Physics of My Homemade Stockfish**: A Nigerian Delicacy, iUniverse, Bloomington, IN, 2025.
2. **Mathmamiya: Loving Mathematics as a Second Language**, iUniverse, Bloomington, IN, 2024.
3. **Wreckless in the City: Physics of Safe Driving for young drivers (and adults too),** iUniverse, Bloomington, Indiana, 2024.
4. **Margin of Death: How close we come each day,** iUniverse, Bloomington, Indiana, 2024
5. **Soccer Greatness at Saint Finbarr's College (Volume II): Legacy of All-Around Sports**, iUniverse, Bloomington, Indiana, 2024

6. **Academics, Discipline, and Sports at Saint Finbarr's College: Tributes to the Great Soccer Players**, iUniverse, Bloomington, Indiana, 2023.
7. **More Physics of Soccer: Playing the Game Smart and Safe,** iUniverse, Bloomington, Indiana, 2022.
8. **Rapidity: Time Management on the Dot**, iUniverse, Bloomington, Indiana, 2022.
9. **The Physics of Skateboarding: Fun, Fellowship, and Following**, iUniverse, Bloomington, Indiana, 2021.
10. **My Everlasting Education at Saint Finbarr's College: Academics, Discipline, and Sports**, iUniverse, Bloomington, Indiana, 2020.
11. **Twenty-Fifth Hour: Secrets to Getting More Done Every Day**, iUniverse, Bloomington, Indiana, 2020.
12. **Kitchen Project Management: The Art and Science of an Organized Kitchen**, iUniverse, Bloomington, Indiana, 2020.
13. **Wives of the Same School: Tributes and Straight Talk**, iUniverse, Bloomington, Indiana, 2019.
14. **The Rooster and the Hen: The Story of Love at Last Look**, iUniverse, Bloomington, Indiana, 2018.
15. **Kitchen Physics: Dynamic Nigerian Recipes**, iUniverse, Bloomington, Indiana, 2018.
16. **The Story of Saint Finbarr's College: Father Slattery's Contributions to Education and Sports in Nigeria,** iUniverse, Bloomington, Indiana, 2018.
17. **Physics of Soccer II: Science and Strategies for a Better Game**, 2018.
18. **Kitchen Dynamics: The Rice Way**, iUniverse, Bloomington, Indiana, 2015.

19. **Consumer Economics: The Value of Dollars and Sense for Money Management**, iUniverse, Bloomington, Indiana, 2015.

20. **Youth Soccer Training Slides: A Math and Science Approach**, iUniverse, Bloomington, Indiana, 2014.

21. **My Little Blue Book of Project Management**, iUniverse, Bloomington, Indiana, 2014.

22. **8 by 3 Paradigm for Time Management**, iUniverse, Bloomington, Indiana, 2013.

23. **Badiru's Equation of Student Success: Intelligence, Common Sense, and Self-Discipline**, iUniverse, Bloomington, Indiana, 2013.

24. **Isi Cookbook: Collection of Easy Nigerian Recipes**, iUniverse, Bloomington, Indiana, 2013.

25. **Blessings of a Father: Education Contributions of Father Slattery at Saint Finbarr's College**, iUniverse, Bloomington, Indiana, 2013.

26. **Physics in the Nigerian Kitchen: The Science, the Art, and the Recipes**, iUniverse, Bloomington, Indiana, 2013.

27. **The Physics of Soccer: Using Math and Science to Improve Your Game**, iUniverse, Bloomington, Indiana, 2010.

28. **Getting Things Done Through Project Management**, iUniverse, Bloomington, Indiana, 2009.

29. **Blessings of a Father: A Tribute to the Life and Work of Reverend Father Denis J. Slattery**, Heriz Designs and Prints, Lagos, Nigeria, 2005.

Dedication

Dedicated to the palate and plate
of all stockfish lovers.

Acknowledgements

I gratefully acknowledge all my family and friends, who have partaken in the products of my homemade stockfish for the past two decades. I would especially like to thank **Chief Olusola Harris** for his extraordinary support, encouragement, and appreciation of my unusual and eclectic pursuit of homemade stockfish, among other professional pursuits. Each harvest season, he has been the first to congratulate me and appreciate my bountiful yield. One of the reasons I continue to make homemade Stockfish is to honor his annual, unwavering support.

I would also like to extend my heartfelt thanks to **Ms. Michaela Finn**, for providing her superb editorial and copyediting services to sanitize this manuscript before it entered the production process. I would also like to thank **Ms. Tunrayo Tawa Jimoh** of Cloud View Concepts, Lagos, Nigeria, who also provided valuable context-related copyediting for this work, and I thank her for her contributions.

Additionally, I am deeply grateful to **Femi and Remi Omitaomu, John and Abidemi Egan, and Ade and**

Deanna Badiru for their immeasurable support for this book (and my other books) by providing me with an efficient, comfortable, quiet, and spacious writing space in each of their homes during family visits. Thank you all for your kindness and hospitality.

About the Front Cover

The front cover is a direct representation of the contents of this book. It shows that we, indeed, judge a book by its cover, regarding what to expect. The cover photo is from my 2024 Stockfish harvest. This beautiful fish is of commercial value and quality, in view, texture, and taste. The raw whole Cod fish (head-on) that turned out this well weighed 15 pounds. It was supplied by the Foremost Seafood Company in Kettering, Ohio, USA, one of my favorite Cod fish supply pipelines. The poundage of the final yield (as shown in the front cover) was 5.5 pounds, before it was consumed into oblivion.

About the Title

The title of this book follows the topical titles of some previous book titles in the ABICS Publications series. Notably, Physics of Soccer, Physics in the Nigerian Kitchen, and Physics of Skateboarding. My website www. PhysicsofSoccer.com states that "Biology determines what we are, Chemistry explains what makes us what we are, and Physics describes what we do." In Stockfish making, chemistry and biology probably play a bigger role than physics as a science. However, figuratively, "physics" of something is often used to refer to how something is done, as in how to execute the logistics and dynamics of making homemade food products. One of my engineering reference books carries the title of "Factory Physics" as a guide for manufacturing enterprises. Reference: **Factory Physics** by Wallace Hopp and Mark Spearman (2008). Factory Physics principles constitute a body of knowledge that relates fundamental manufacturing measures such as cycle time, throughput, capacity, work-in-process, inventory, and variability. Winner of the 1998, IIE Book of the Year Award, Factory Physics: Foundations of Manufacturing Management, is a comprehensive introduction to manufacturing management that starts with an overview of historical practices and then develops a framework of fundamental principles that comprehensively describe the natural behavior at work in factory operations. The authors describe 22 Laws for Manufacturing that help managers better understand, control and optimize performance of their factories. In essence, factory physics is "a systematic description of the underlying behavior of manufacturing systems. Understanding it enables managers and engineers to work with the natural tendencies of manufacturing systems to

1. Identify opportunities for improving existing systems.
2. Design effective new systems.
3. Make the tradeoffs needed to coordinate policies from disparate areas

Ditto for the theme and premise of this book.

Now, you may proceed with the physics of my homemade Stockfish.

The image below shows the cover of a previous physics-based ABICS publications book.

The Science, the Art, and the Recipes

Deji Badiru
Iswat Badiru

PHYSICS
IN THE
NIGERIAN KITCHEN

My Homemade Stockfish

Yes, I make homemade stockfish. Why is this strange? While I did some research about Stockfish and the process of making it, some readers may be unaware of this. So proving some context, just a paragraph or two, will help clear up any bewilderment that readers may have, while also providing them with new knowledge.

As far as I know, I am the only one who engages in this unusual annual winter pursuit, just for the sake of fun, science, and private consumption.

In my professional profile and curriculum vitae, "kitchen science experiments" prominently features among my avocations.

It has been and continues to be a labor of love and passion of seeing whole raw cod fish transformed into the rock-hard stockfish through a science-based drying and fermentation or curing process. For years, many who have tasted my homemade stockfish products have encouraged me to transform it into a money-making venture because of the highly coveted and pricey commodity. I have refused to engage in the art and science of homemade Stockfish as a business because doing so would rob me of the joy of making the stockfish and giving it away free as a savory gift to my close family and friends, for their personal enjoyment.

I first ventured into the experiment of making Stockfish at home in Knoxville, Tennessee in 2001. At the time, I was the Department Head of Industrial Engineering at the University of Tennessee. My family had moved from the University of Oklahoma in Norman, Oklahoma in 2000. One weekend, in my usual (then and now) "legs-on" approach to seeing what is going on town, particularly in stores, I stopped at Oriental Super Mart on Sutherland Avenue in Knoxville. "Legs-on" is my own connotation (similar to hands-on) for going somewhere in person. I spotted a strange-looking fish head-on. "Head-on" is the way fish marketers describe fish with its head on. I didn't know what it was because the label on the packaging was written in some Asian language. Google translate was not prevalent then, or else I would have searched for the English name of the fish. Nonetheless, I decided to buy it as an object for one of my kitchen-science taste experiments. I didn't know it would later become an object of my affection. At home, I cooked the fish as my family would normally cook Tilapia and Catfish in a Nigeria stew or soup. It tasted terrible. Neither my wife nor I cared for the rotten undertone of the taste. I thought the taste had a hint of familiar stockfish, so, I decided to investigate further. My investigation did not immediately include buying more of the fish because my wife (my Lovely Dear Iswat) had mandated that "thou shalt not buy that same rotten fish again." So, I restricted my investigation and research to a paper study. With the hint of stockfish that I could discern in the cooked fish, I began studying how Stockfish was made in Norway. In Nigeria, it was (and still is) common knowledge that all Stockfish imports originated from Norway. My discovery was astounding and astonishing. Stockfish is, actually, a Cod fish that has gone through the process of natural air drying. I said to myself then, as a researcher by profession, "I must duplicate that process."

I began reflecting. Cod fish must be versatile and I recalled that a product called "Cod liver oil" was popular in Nigeria at that time. Could it be from the same Cod fish that I am experimenting with? I would later find out that Cod liver is a food product that has various health benefits. It contains essential fatty acids that help prevent blood clotting, reduce pain and swelling, and lower high blood pressure. It also provides vitamins that support the immune, reproductive, hormonal, and nervous systems, as well as the skin, heart, and blood vessels. Cod liver oil is a supplement that may help relieve joint stiffness, improve cardiovascular health, and repair damaged teeth, nails, hair, and skin. It sounded to me then that Cod was the king of fish.

Soon after concluding my research, I went back to the oriental store and bought more of the strange-looking fish, head-on. Knowing what the head-side of a commercial Stockfish looked like, I first experimented and discovered how to cut the fish head off to create the unique oblong shape that we see on Stockfish. It is not a straight cutoff process. The head is cut off in an angled and triangular maneuvering of the butcher knife. I made the cut! That was a triumph. Now, what should I do with the head-off fish? Knowing that commercial Stockfish often have a string attached to the dried fish tail. I figured out that the string was used to hand the fish upside down. My research result was panning out well. So, I went and bought metal hooks. I hung each whole head-off Cod Fish upside down on the railings of the wooden deck behind our house on 12116 Broadwood Drive, Farragut (Knoxville), Tennessee.

It was in the middle of a hot summer. I naively thought the intense hot summer heat would dry the Cod fish easily. Wrong! Two things happened:

1. Instead of drying in the open intense heat of the summer, the fish quickly got rotten, and unconsumable. The delectable aroma (which many people find disgusting) was evident in the rotten fish. I knew I was on the brink of a new avocation pursuit. So, I would not give up. I would later discover that drying Cod fish is a winter time affair.
2. On the open deck, wild animals thought I hung the fish out there for their easy picking, and pick and nibble, they did, indeed. So, many of my rotten fish were in tattered pieces from the gnawing teeth of

wild animals. I was not deterred. I would later learn to build a custom cage within which my Cod fish would reside and be unreachable to wild animals, probably neighborhood feral cats. Luckily ferocious bears were not in our Knoxville neighborhood. Bears are notorious for being able to get into anything to reach any food item.

Harvest sample of Deji-made Stockfish

My Cod Fish Supply Chain

Finding and retaining my whole cod fish supply pipeline has been tough. Ever since I first bought the first whole Cod fish, I have been vigilant to find other stores or sources for whole Cod Fish head-on. It is a rare commodity, hardly found in stores. Fish stores may carry cod fillets and cod chunks, but never the whole cod. Whole cod fish with head-on looks ugly and unappetizing, usually with mouth agape. No store would want to drive away customers with the sight of an ugly fish. Unable to find another regular source, I have purchased whole cod fish head-on from the same Oriental Super Mart in Knoxville every year. That's 23 years straight as of 2024. Most times, it is by special orders rather than a drop-in purchase. Knoxville is a five-hour drive from Dayton, Ohio. After we moved from Knoxville to Ohio, I have made the trip religiously every year to get my order of whole cod fish head-on from Knoxville. It is always like an annual pilgrimage from Dayton, Ohio to Knoxville, Tennessee.

My long-time whole Cod fish supplier:
Oriental Super Mart (https://www.facebook.com/
OrientalSuperMart/)
3800 Sutherland Ave, Knoxville, TN 37919

After a multi-year relentless search and pursuit, I discovered in 2023 a seafood company that could order whole cod fish (head-on) for me from New England states. Thus, I added another Cod fish supply pipeline. The company is located in Dayton, Ohio. My specific requirement is by a special order, which arrives professionally ice-packed in two or three days.

My additional whole Cod fish supplier:
Foremost Seafood (www.foremostseafood.com)
1912 Woodman Center Dr, Kettering, OH 45420

The good thing about the Foremost seafood order is that I can request the fish be gutted and cleaned before shipment, of course at an additional cost. The Oriental Super Mart orders come without gutting or cleaning. It is always a monumental, dirty, and long process to clean Cod fish at home. My wife says I am the only one crazy enough to embark on such buying and cleaning of cod fish, just for the sake of continuing a kitchen science experiment. But, she, nonetheless, each year quickly digs into my harvest stockpile (of Stockfish) to cook our favorite savory Nigerian dishes. Eating is easier than cleaning, so she proclaims.

Whichever way that I can purchase whole Cod fish head-on, it is always a terribly expensive proposition. However, it is my irrevocable avocation task that must be done every year, taking advantage of the cold winter months, running, typically, from November through April in my region of the USA (Dayton, Ohio, USA).

Those who have ever seen whole Cod fish head-on (mouth agape) always remember how ugly this head is. In the early days, I used to discard (and trash) the heads after surgically removing them from the body. Around 2005, I had a Nigerian student, Mr. Godswill Nsofor, a native of Eastern Nigeria, where Stockfish consumption was particular of a high culinary tradition, who expressed interest in having the decapitated Stockfish heads for personal consumption. Godswill was unmarried then and, as an international student on limited funds, he needed a boost of his ethnic food options. He, gleefully, carted away the fresh heads of my stash of whole Cod fish. After Godswill graduated with his Masters Degree in Industrial Engineering and my family moved from Tennessee to Ohio, I started retaining the Cod fish heads for my own further experimentations. I, now, occasionally cook the heads, dry them, or give them away to those who favor them as savory items. So goes one "Deji-Vu" story of the Cod fish head. Deji-Vu (a play on Déjà vu) is how some close friends and associates describe my frequent fish stories.

Some close observers wonder why I go through the trouble of making Stockfish at home when I can just go to the store and buy the imported commercial Stockfish directly. Some think it is a matter of the cost reduction of homemade products. Some think it is due to the convenience of making things at home. Some think it is the ready accessibility to what you make yourself at home. Some think it is a safeguard against unsafe food products from unknown sources. None of these is true. I embark upon this tedious pursuit purely for fun and the proving ground of food science. When I factor in the cost of buying the whole cod fish and the tremendous amount of my time and labor put into the homemade process, it ends up costing me more per pound than just buying Stockfish in the store. There is an innate joy of making rather than buying. By the way, commercial Stockfish is available via amazon.com at a cost of roughly $25 per pound.

Quiz:

Which countries import stockfish from Norway?

Stockfish is exported from Norway to over 30 countries including Italy, Sweden, Germany, UK, France, Spain, USA, Nigeria, Cameroon, and others.

The Stockfish Trade Agreement

This section presents an interesting account of the long-ago Stockfish Trade Agreement between Nigeria and Norway. In his 1954 book entitled, "The West African Trade," P. T. Bauer narrated that in the 1930's and from 1946 to 1951, the bulk of Norwegian Stockfish imported into Nigeria was covered by an agreement between the National Association of Norwegian Stockfish Exporters, a statutory organization, whose members alone had the right to export Stockfish, and a group of West African import merchants. The existence of the agreement and its broad outline were widely known and were the subject of frequent complaints in West Africa. The agreement was abandoned in 1951. Its operation presented some features of interest of special relevance to a study of marketing arrangements in a trade in which there is a comparatively high degree of concentration both among the suppliers and the distributors. The trade in Stockfish ("panla" in the Nigerian Yoruba language and "okporoko" in the Nigerian Igbo language) can be traced to as far back as the 1880s. P. T. Bauer described the Norwegian Stockfish as "a commodity, which is an important staple line in the Nigerian import trade." This is another testament to the justification for my writing about my homemade Stockfish experimentations.

Reference: P. T. Bauer (1954), **West African Trace: A Study of Competition, Oligopoly and Monopoly in a Changing Economy**, Cambridge University Press, London, UK.

If a "changing economy" was addressed in 1954, I wonder what P. T. Bauer would have written about the radically-changed economy of today.

My Fish Stories

As a brief digression, I recount here some of my most hilarious fish stories.

First: In 1996, a colleague of mine at New Jersey Institute of Technology, Professor Layek Abdel-Malek, recounted to our other colleagues his experience in observing me go to a Seattle Fish Market, where I purchased the biggest ocean-caught Salmon available. The Salmon was packaged, iced, and stored in my hotel room overnight for my early-morning flight out of Seattle back to Oklahoma City. I was teaching at the University of Oklahoma then. I attended the annual Operations Research Conference in Seattle. Which was when Professor Abdel-Malek and I crossed paths again, after knowing each other for many years prior to the conference. For many years, Professor Abdel-Malek took delight in mentioning this Salmon fish encounter to our other colleagues. He found it fascinating that a well-known scholar would subject himself to wrestling a big package of fresh Salmon out of Seattle back to Oklahoma. Of course, I was proud of the accomplishment because not many other fish lovers could have done that. Unfortunately, this was in the days before cell phone cameras came along. So, there is no photographic documentation of the sight and size of my Seattle Salmon fish.

Second: This is a Deji-Vu repeat of my big fish story. The full re-narration (as originally presented on January 29, 2023) goes as follows.

Well, my plan yesterday (Saturday, January 28, 2023) was to be a good boy and stay home and write and write, right from the beginning of the day.

But the weather was good and I decided to take advantage of nature by venturing out, cruising the local stores in search of unscheduled opportunities to contribute to local economic development.

My wife did not want to go out, so I was free to roam the stores unrestrained, as I wished.

I stumbled onto a fish store and I saw this massive fish of about my size. The store had never carried such a sight before. Only on TV have I seen such a large fish, except for when my wife and I visited the old traditional fish market in Tokyo several years ago, while visiting my former University of Oklahoma Japanese student, Mr. Masayuki Nakada.

Unbeknownst to me and unprompted by me, my sense of a "new kitchen science experiment" kicked in, upon the sight of this massive fish. I must conquer this fish and show who is the boss of new kitchen challenges.

The store owners were puzzled why I would want all that fish (whole) to myself. Normally, they would cut it into pieces to sell to multiple customers, using their industrial saw. They wondered how I would cut the fish at home. I told them not to worry, I was well equipped for the challenge. They didn't know whom they were dealing it. They didn't know that I was originally from Epe, Lagos State, Nigeria. They didn't know I had all kinds of kitchen cutting tools, some of them sharp enough to cut off a finger.

Even the store cashier had a hard time wrestling the fish onto their tiny checkout counter scale. I had to intervene to show her my industrial engineering trick of weighing objects larger than the scale. The other shoppers in the checkout line had fun watching and wondering about the cashier-fish-shopper tussle. Even packaging the paid-for fish was a dilemma. I went into the store's back room (yes, I did) and I found an empty box, huge and strong enough to handle the task. Everyone clapped and laughed about my tenacity to have this big fish (whole), no matter what.

After arriving at home and wrestling the big fish box from my GMC Terrain SUV, I brought out all my kitchen gadgets. My wife was inside the house, wondering why I was shuttling in and out of the garage and the basement storage. I did not immediately tell her what was about to unfold. If she saw the huge uncleaned fish upfront, she would have been alarmed and would send me back to the store to return the fish. So, I kept the secret to myself while doing the deal of fish cleaning. Luckily, she did not come into the garage during the dirty part of my "sausage making" (aka fish cleaning).

I only called her for the photo session after the fish, a rare Carp, was cleaned and presentable. She could only laugh and commiserate with me for my self-imposed ordeal. Thankfully, she did not refuse to help me with the photo session. I had thought of covertly taking a selfie with the fish, thereby preserving the secrecy, but the fish was too big and too heavy for a one-handed selfie. I guess a tripod and the camera timing would have worked, but that would only add to my oppressive struggle. Needless to say, I give photo credit to my wife for the "fish and me" poster.

After the photo documentary was done, I enlisted the services of my trusted industrial saw (yeah, I have some saws that I no longer trust) to do the slicing and cut-off chores. The rest is history, as you see in the last photo of the documentary. Oh yes, I pressed two of my three garage-residing commercial-grade air fryers into service to do the thermodynamic heat transfer process. The sight of the result is glaring and appealingly appetizing. Enjoy the sight even if you cannot be present to partake in the consumption.

Everything worked out perfectly and I conquered the colossal carp. The kitchen deal is done.

My Big Carp Fish and Me: January 28, 2023

Third: This is a testimony of how I seem to always be in a place and position to snap a good photo of fish scenes. The photo below is what I snapped at the Olumo Fish Market of Epe, Lagos State, Nigeria, where I hailed from. This was in 2017 during a vacation visit to Epe, which is seen as the fish capital of Lagos State, Nigeria.

Fourth: For many years, I have, periodically, roasted Tilapia fish under a moniker that I call "Eja Epe," meaning fish from Epe (Lagos, State, Nigeria). This is, actually, a comedic salutatory recognition of my hometown of Epe. The Tilapia that I use are, really, commercial Tilapia from regular fish stores in my city of residence. While in Florida, Oklahoma, and Tennessee. I mostly used charcoal grille. In Ohio, I started with charcoal grilles also. But the advent of modern Air Fryer appliances caused me to shift to that source of roasting Tilapia. I regularly give the roasted Tilapia to friends and family as presents. I often joke that Eja Epe is a panacea for all types of ailments. If someone gets sick, I make Eja Epe for them as a "get-well-quick" stimulant.

Scene from Epe Fish Market
Photo Credit: Deji Badiru, 2017

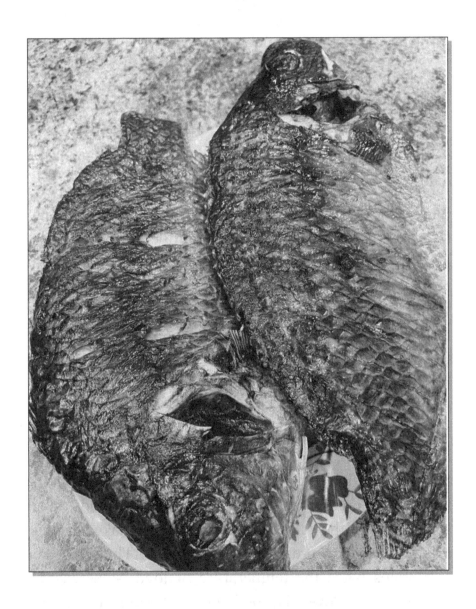

Science of Food Drying

Back to the Cod fish task at hand. Drying of food, including fish, has existed in human history for millennia. Indigenous people in many parts of the world have documented records of air-drying food. Decreasing the amount of water in the food inhibits deleterious microorganisms from developing and spoiling the food. The drying of Cod fish, in particular, has existed in the food export history of Norway (in Scandinavia) for ages. Almost all of the imported commercial Stockfish in the markets of Nigeria come from Norway. Once I made this linkage in my research, I could narrow my focus on homemade Stockfish drying. Drying food removes moisture from it, inhibiting the growth of bacteria, yeasts, and molds, thus slowing down the action of enzymes. This makes drying an effective food preservation technique. The moisture evaporates when the temperature of food is increased, and air moving over the food carries the moisture away. A balance of temperature and humidity is needed to successfully dry foods. Dehydration is one of the most common methods for preserving all the most popular fruits and vegetables, along with meat and herbs. This process removes 85-95% of the moisture in your food.

Although there are several methods, gadgets, and techniques for drying food, Cod fish is simply air dried. No salt is applied. No ingredients are injected. Nature simply does its job on the fish. After experimenting with different types of fish, only Cod fish (and its family, including haddock, whiting, and pollock) possess the natural properties to become Stockfish after drying. Other types of fish will dry well, depending on the method used, but they don't yield our traditional Stockfish. What I also discovered through my personal experimental research is that Cod fish fillets don't dry to become the traditional Stockfish. Neither does chunk (cut pieces) of Cod fish. Skinned Cod fish also does not dry to become the traditional Stockfish. Scientifically, there must be something in the skin-on mode of Cod fish that aids the controlled fermentation process in the cycle of Cod fish to Stockfish. I will let food scientists worry about such details.

For the purpose of this book, "drying" is the removal of water from any material, such as a food item. This may be done by means of exposing the food to heated air in a chamber (a dryer) or it may be accomplished through natural means, such as solar drying, where the sun provides the energy necessary to remove the water from the food. The newer home appliance sold as "air fryers" use heated air to cook (rather than dry) food. For the purpose of my homemade Stockfish, simple air drying without salt, oil, or anything else is what I use.

Reasons for Drying Foods

- Spoilage reduction
- Enhanced storage life
- Changed storage conditions
- Weight reduction
- Increased convenience
- Changed properties

Methods of Water Removal and Dehydration

- Traditional methods
- Non-traditional methods

Factors Influencing Drying

- Product attributes
- Size and dimensions
- Particle size
- Particle shape
- Composition, structure, and porosity
- Initial moisture content
- Surface characteristics
- Specific surface area

- Specific heat capacity
- Seasonal variation (winter, summer, autumn)
- Cultivar (farm raised, cultivated, variety)
- Drying equipment attributes
- Type of dryer
- Dryer design features
- Air temperature
- Retention times
- Ambient relative humidity
- Volumetric air flowrate
- Linear air velocity
- Air flow patterns
- Seasonal and daily variations

Effects of Drying on Products

- Nutritional alteration (e.g., Degradation)
- Structural integrity (e.g., loss of outline and profile)
- Change in culinary functionality (reduction or augmentation)
- Flavor and aroma changes (enhancement or reduction)
- Color changes (appealing or masking)
- Hardening (handling and packaging)
- Release of soluble constituents

Cod Fish Fermentation Process

Basically, fermentation impacts a pungent odor to foods. In Stockfish, that pungent odor is a desirable and appetizing aroma. The word fermentation comes from the Latin word *fervere*, which means "to boil." Technically, fermentation "boils" the molecules of food through the action of bacteria. Yes, bacteria, that notorious organism that we love to hate, but still needed for many desirable processes in our day-to-day lives.

Fermentation (controlled spoilage) is what gives Stockfish its strong aroma, which outsiders may consider as disgusting rotten smell. It is all in the aroma perspective of each individual. One person's rotten smell is another person's desirable culinary aroma. Yes, Stockfish takes getting used to, for the uninitiated outsiders. The aroma of Stockfish is unique, strong, and long lasting. It is like skunk on steroids. An interesting story about this happened to my wife while we were in Norman, Oklahoma, long before I started doing my homemade Stockfish. In those days, a group of our Nigerian families used to get together to order bales of Stockfish from a supplier in Los Angeles, California. The supplier then, Mr. Sunday Nyenke, had been a long-time family friend from our initial days at Tennessee Technological University in Cookeville, Tennessee. He relocated to Los Angeles, where he and his wife operated a Nigerian food supply store. Sunday would order bales of the highly-desired Stockfish from Norway and ship them to Nigerian buyers across the USA. This was around 1988 to 1990. I was teaching at the University of Oklahoma. My wife was concurrently working in the Office of the Provost at the University. One day, I was already at work when our ordered bale of Stockfish arrived at our home address, before my wife left for work. The bale was dropped by the outside door by the delivery truck. When my wife stepped out to go to work and she saw the delivered bale, about 70 pounds of cargo, she simply dragged the bale inside, without opening it, and went on to work. She recounted that as soon as she got to work, coworkers started remarking that someone had brought some rotten fish meal to the office. They couldn't find the source. They set about spraying disinfectants and odor neutralizers around the office. My wife, of course, quickly realized that she was the source of the "sweet aroma," but she could not fess up to the coworkers about what had happened. She quickly took an excuse and went back home to take a shower and change clothes. So, strong was the smell of the baled Stockfish that even touching the bale packaging externally transferred the odious smell to her hands and clothes. Traditionally, the stronger the Stockfish aroma, the higher the quality of the Stockfish. Thank you, Mr. Fermentation.

Although most people are familiar with fermentation in the context of the production of alcohol, the fermentation of food is widely embraced throughout the world.

Fermentation is an ancient technique for preserving food.

Fermentation is the anaerobic breakdown of molecules such as glucose by yeasts, bacteria, or plants. It is a chemical process by which molecules such as glucose are broken down anaerobically. More broadly, fermentation is the foaming that occurs during the manufacture of wine and beer, a process at least 10,000 years old. The frothing results from the evolution of carbon dioxide gas, though this was not recognized until the 17th century. French chemist and microbiologist Louis Pasteur (of the pasteurization fame) in the 19th century used the term fermentation in a narrow sense to describe the changes brought about by yeasts and other microorganisms growing in the absence of air (anaerobically); he also recognized that ethyl alcohol and carbon dioxide are not the only products of fermentation.

In chemistry and biology, fermentation is a biochemical process that obtains energy from carbohydrates without using oxygen. Many foods come from fermentation, which has many industrial applications.

While organisms use fermentation mainly for energy, people apply the process for making many products, including the following:

- Beer
- Wine
- Mead (Honey wine)
- Liquor
- Cheese
- Yogurt
- Leavened bread
- Sourdough bread.
- Industrial alcohol (for biofuels)
- Sour food containing lactic acid, such as kimchi, sauerkraut, pickles, pepperoni, and Stockfish (the subject of this book)

Fermented foods may reduce heart disease risk and aid digestion, immunity, and weight loss.

Fermented foods, in spite of their repulsive odors, are rich in beneficial probiotics and have been associated with a range of health benefits, from better digestion to a stronger immunity.

Yes, fermentation is all around us, in various forms. Sewage treatment involves fermentation. Human muscles initially use aerobic respiration, but switch to fermentation and produce lactic acid as an anaerobic energy supply. Bacteria in the human digestive tract perform fermentation, producing hydrogen gas and sometimes methane as flatus (farts).

On the cautionary side, fermented foods are considered safe for most people. However, some individuals may experience adverse side effects, depending on the source and magnitude. Due to the high probiotic content of fermented foods, the most common side effect is an initial and temporary increase in gas and bloating. These symptoms may be worse after consuming fiber-rich fermented foods, such as kimchi and sauerkraut. It's also important to note that not all fermented foods are created equal. Some products may contain high levels of added sugar, salt, and fat. I note here that my homemade Stockfish does not have any "added" anything.

One caution is to avoid incorrect temperatures, fermentation duration, or unsterile equipment, which can cause the food to spoil and become unsafe to eat. I note here that once I made my experimental discovery, I only make my homemade Stockfish in the appropriate winter temperatures of Ohio.

In a social sense, fermentation adds *tang*, *zing*, and *zest* to food products. These effects are often unforgettable, both to those who embrace them and those who detest them.

By the way, fermentation and curing are often confused or use interchangeably. Food scientists make a clear distinction between both. In my own simple-minded operational understanding, fermentation is a natural process that happens from within the interior of the food item itself while curing is externally driven through the addition of external agents, such as salt, pickles, sugar, spices, and so on. If we consider the impact of sunlight heat as an external agent, then fermentation is a form of curing, in the functional sense.

Curing is any of various food preservation and flavoring processes of foods such as meat, fish and vegetables, by the addition of salt, with the aim of drawing moisture out of the food by the process of osmosis. Because curing increases the solute concentration in the food and hence decreases its water potential, the food becomes inhospitable for the microbe growth that causes food spoilage. Curing can be traced back to antiquity. It was the primary method of preserving meat and fish until the late 19th century. Dehydration was the earliest form of food curing. Many curing processes also involve smoking, spicing, cooking, or the addition of combinations of sugar, nitrate, and nitrite.

There is a lot of technicalities involved in the biology, chemistry, physics, and dynamics of fermentation. Before getting too carried away, I will stop here for now, so that I can get to my favorite topic of making my homemade Stockfish.

My Art
of Homemade
Stockfish

One of my favorite avocations is my "kitchen science experiments." If you think engineering and kitchen don't go together, you are very wrong. Please read on.

By now, you know why I got into the act of homemade Stockfish. You also know when, on an annual basis, I get into the routine. Below is how I do it. It is simple process. Once get through the rigmarole of buying and cleaning whole Cod fish, I simply hang them out to air dry in my custom-built wooden cage around the middle of November. The cage has a fine wire mesh around the four sides to prevent flies from getting in easily, while allowing a free air flow from all four directions. On the top, a place a horizontal glass panel which allows sunlight to pass through for radiated heat to do the drying process. For me and my home location, my desirable weather day would be dry, sunny, and windy, with temperatures just above the freezing point, but below 40 degrees Fahrenheit. If it is too consistently below the freezing point for an extended period, the fish would freeze. If it is too consistently hot for an extended period, the fish would rot. As I mentioned in an earlier paragraph, the skin on the Cod fish has such unique properties that the drying process and the fermentation process are balanced within some margin of error to yield the appropriate Stockfish product. Without the skin the Cod fish flesh will rot before getting to the drying stage. Once I hang the fish upside down by the stringed tail, I don't do anything else until harvest time around the middle of April the following year. I occasionally check on the cage to ensure everything is in order, such as the cage's structural integrity and the condition of the glass top. If the temperature sours prematurely, some dark maggot organism will start developing within the flesh of the fish. For this reason, harvesting at the right time is very essential. If left for a prolonged period of time, when no further drying is happening, the crawling micro living organism will start messing with the fish flesh from the inside. If harvested too soon before the interior dries and hardens, the interior flesh will start getting rotten. If harvesting is not done properly the timely, the intense heat of the summer will not provide any additional drying. Instead, it will create a fertile ground for micro living organisms to thrive.

Nigerians and Their Craving

To better understand the Stockfish craving that Nigerians have, readers are referred to the several online posting about the topic. YouTube Videos abound to provide educational and interesting accounts and encounters of Stockfish-based meals and recipes. Many videos are very accurate and provide credence to the labor of love in my recreational experimentations with homemade Stockfish production.

One good YouTube Video Source is

https://www.youtube.com/watch?v=1CHt6Yo6sV.

If it is no longer available at the time of reading this, there are many other options that can be found.

It is a fun thing for me to do, but my main challenges are finding the fresh whole cod fish and having cold enough weather for the slow drying process.

Manually cleaning and gutting the raw cod fish is a messy and laborious process that not many people can stand.

Finding the raw cod fish to buy is an extremely expensive proposition. It is the excitement of the science behind the process that remains my motivation for continuation, just as an avid golfer will continue to pour money into his game, again and again, even if no income is derived from the sport.

Options for Using Cod Fish Head

An old Turkish expression says "A fish always begins to rot at the head." It is a reference to leadership values. This axiom can be equally applied to many organizational scenarios.

Through my kitchen experiments, I have concluded that there are several options for using the Cod fish head. I present five options below:

1. You can discard them, which is what many Western fish processing companies would do. This is a waste and not a desirable option in an ethnic culture.
2. You can cook the heads as a delicious Nigerian fish pepper soup. Don't make the soup too peppery so that it can be savored and enjoyed. The bone structure in the Cod head is soft and can chewed while sucking the juicy soup sauce from the inner nooks and cranial corners of the head. This makes for a savory finger-licking experience.

3. You can fry the heads lightly in vegetable oil and eat them (with your hands) as a snack or an appetizer. This goes great with a bottle of chilled palm wine.

4. You can air fry them for a crunchy snack. Since there is not much fish flesh in the Cod head, air frying takes away the juiciness of the fried output. Air frying uses the natural liquid or oil in the food to achieve the cooking. Cod head does not have much flesh. Thus, air frying produces more of a crunchy snack than a juicy munch.

5. If you don't want to go through the trouble of cooking the Cod heads yourself, you can give them away to appreciative friends, family, or neighbors, who are familiar with the culinary value of Stockfish.

Youtube site to see

Rozy's Kitchen has an excellent Youtube video of how to cook Stockfish. I recommend visiting the site:

https://www.youtube.com/watch?v=wJxY92qZ7wA&t=48s

Instagram: @lifewithrozy

Twitter: @Lifewithrozy

Stockfish drying in Norway

During my Stockfish research over the years, I came across many useful references. One very helpful source in the Instagram link shown below.

Reference: Instagram Video (How stockfish is dried in Norway)

https://www.instagram.com/reel/CuUTuz-g_nj/?igshid= NjFhOGMzYTE3ZQ%3D%3D

The name **Stockfish** is derived from **"stick fish,"** because of the wooden frames on which it is dried. It is cured in the open air over several weeks (in Norway), typically from February, when the season opens, to April. Then, to keep the spring rains from spoiling it, it's brought indoors to finish drying. By midsummer it's fully cured, and ready to be graded and sold for export. It takes three months for cod to fully dry and become stockfish. In my own homemade process, I run the drying process for about five months. In Norway, the fish is dried on large drying racks in a dry and airy environment for about three months, between January and April. During the drying process, about 80% of the water in the fish evaporates. The ideal drying conditions are found in Lofoten and Finmarken, Norway. Coincidentally, the production duration is the time of the year when Codfish comes to the coast to spawn.

The popularity of Lofoten for Stockfish making is similar to the popularity of Epe, Lagos State, Nigeria for general fish products.

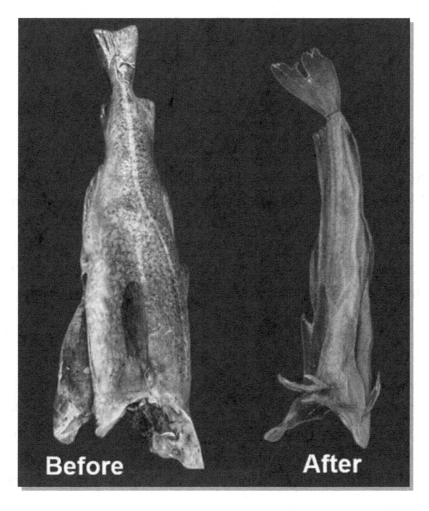

How Dried Cod Became a Norwegian Staple and an Italian Delicacy

By Roff Smith, February, 7, 2020

Source: https://www.atlasobscura.com/articles/norway-italy-dried-cod-trade-stockfish (Reprinted with permission)

The lucrative stockfish trade dates back to the Viking days. Norwegians, including the indigenous Sámi, have been drying cod for centuries.

It's 11 o'clock on a dim, cold, blustery morning in February, with a feeble arctic sun barely peeping over the horizon, and the harbor at Røstlandet is a hive of activity. Three boats are tied up to the wharf, delivering their bounties of fresh caught cod, while the skipper of another boat nestles his craft into a slot freshly vacated by a fourth. Ropes are cast, and cranes swing into operation. Through the open doors of a fish factory, forklifts can be seen shunting around the concrete floor, bearing huge plastic tubs filled with cod, cod livers, and salted cod roe.

Back on the dock, sales are made and deals are struck with a handshake, in an atmosphere of hard, cheery camaraderie. Some of these men have known each other since they were schoolboys together, watching their fathers and grandfathers doing these very same things.

It's cod season once again in the far north of Norway, and Røst—a remote scatter of rocky islets off the outermost tip of Norway's Lofoten Islands—is once more the honeypot for fishermen seeking jackpot paychecks in the lucrative dried cod trade, Norway's oldest export industry, dating back to the Viking days.

Every winter, for more than a thousand years, Norwegian fishermen have flocked to these parts to scoop up the bounty of big, meaty migrating cod that come streaming down by the millions from the Barents Sea to breed among the reefs and shoals around the Lofoten Islands, and most especially here around Røst.

The fish are cleaned and gutted and hung by their tails, in pairs, to dry in the traditional manner, on slatted wooden frames that can be seen all over the island. Then the catch is rendered into stockfish—the nutritious cod jerky that once sustained the Vikings on their long sea voyages and, today, is a highly prized delicacy in Italy, where it's a key ingredient in traditional regional dishes from Venice, Naples, Genoa, and Calabria.

"Stockfish isn't an Italian product, but sometimes you could almost imagine that it was," says Olaf Pedersen, a former CEO of Glea Sjømat, one of Røst's main stockfish companies, founded by his grandfather in 1936. "Over the centuries it has become deeply ingrained into their culinary and cultural traditions."

Indeed, the Ligurian town of Badalucco holds a stockfish festival every year to commemorate the time, back in the Middle Ages, when the townspeople survived a siege by Moorish invaders by eating only stockfish. And over near Venice, on the opposite side of the country, the town of Sandrigo hosts the world's largest stockfish festival—the Festa del Bacalà, held every September in celebration of the famed regional dish Baccalà alla Vicentina.

So important is the Italian market to Norway's stockfish producers that Pedersen recently moved from Røst to Milan, where he now looks after the interests of a collective of 22 stockfish producers. Lofoten stockfish was recently awarded Denomination of Origin status, meaning it enjoys the same legal protections as Parma ham and French champagne.

Any way you want to measure it, it's a long way from the warm Mediterranean sunshine to the moody skies over Røst, whose 365 islets and skerries are home to a few hundred hardy Norwegians and about a million seabirds. Yet the links between these two very different places go back nearly 600 years, to the shipwreck in 1432 of a Venetian merchant trader named Pietro Quirini. After his boat sank, he spent three enjoyable months with the islanders, and on his return to Italy, presented an account of his adventures to the Venetian senate.

Stockfish festivals abound in Italy, where dried cod has been a part of the culinary culture for nearly 600 years.

He also brought back some stockfish. The rich, nutritious, intensely flavored cod jerky proved an instant culinary hit, finding its way into regional dishes all over the country. An improbable new trade route was born, linking the Renaissance city states then comprising Italy with the lonely windswept isles of Røst.

It's a trade route that's helped make the islanders rich: Røst has the highest per capita number of millionaires in Norway. And the Italian historical connection persists. Take a stroll through Røst today and you'll come upon places with names like the Quirini Cafe and Quirini Park. In 2012, an opera based on Quirini's shipwreck premiered on Røst—a first for the tiny island—and was so popular with locals and visitors that it was brought back for a repeat performance two years later.

The islanders owe their good fortune to their unique location. Not only does Nature deliver countless millions of migrating cod to their doorstep every winter. Thanks to the modifying effects of the Gulf Stream, they also enjoy exceptionally mild winters, given their latitude. Although the island sits well above the Arctic Circle, at nearly 68° north, winter temperatures here seldom fall much below freezing, or rise much above it.

"We have the perfect climate for making stockfish," says Pedersen. "It's a fine line. Even a couple of degrees can make all the difference. If the temperature were to fall to, say, minus-3 [degrees Celsius, or 26 degrees Fahrenheit], the freezing action breaks down the cells in the flesh, and you end up with something that's yellowish and rubbery and unpalatable.

On the other hand, if the temperature rises too high, you'll just get a slow rot."

Whether Røst's delicately balanced climate stays perfect for making stockfish is an open question. So is the effect warmer waters might have on cod migration routes. One change that has already been noticed in a warming world is that fishing villages elsewhere in Lofoten that were previously too cold for making stockfish are now able to do so. "Røst doesn't have it all to itself quite so much any more," says Pedersen. Each cod is assigned one of 20 different grades based on subtleties in color, texture, and scent.

"Stockfish is like fine cognac," says Ansgar Pedersen, a veteran cod grader at Glea Sjømat who has been in the business all his life. Now nearly 70 years old, he has no plans to retire anytime soon. "I'll retire when I'm 80," he says with a laugh. He loves his job, which is just as well, as it requires him to examine each of the 400,000 or so dried cod the company sells each year, holding the fish up to the light, looking for subtleties in color, texture, and scent before deciding which of the 20 different grades to assign it.

Once or twice a year he'll travel to Italy to meet with buyers and discuss their needs. "The people in Naples tend to want larger, meatier cod than those in Genoa or Calabria," he says. "It all depends on how they are preparing. Each region has their own specialty."

If stockfish has insinuated itself into Italian culture and cuisine, it's the very warp and weft of Norwegian. "There is a taste of cod in all my music," Norwegian composer Edvard Grieg once claimed. It's a coda that can be said to run through the rest of Norway's culture and history as well, with the iconic fish appearing on crests and coats of arms in cities and villages up and down the coast.

The earliest literary reference to the dried-cod trade comes in an almost operatic scene in Egil's Saga, a Viking yarn set in the ninth century. In it, a young Norse raider named Thorolf Kvendulfsson sets off for England in a brilliantly painted, dragon-prowed vessel, its blue- and red-striped sail filling with the summer breeze, its thwarts piled high with the fortune in furs and dried cod he and his men had accumulated during the previous winter.

The cargo fetches a fancy price in England, and Thorolf returns to Norway a wealthy man, only to fall afoul of the king, who feels that Thorolf has been getting a little too rich, a little too cocky, and not paying his taxes. Their subsequent falling out—and Thorolf's murder—sets up an intergenerational feud that forms the narrative thread of one of the greatest of the Old Norse sagas.

By the time 13th-century scribes got around to committing the tale to parchment, the stockfish trade in which Thorolf had been dabbling had become the economic engine for the whole of Norway, accounting for more than 80 percent of the country's exports, and a source of immense wealth. With medieval Europe's population rapidly growing and urbanizing, there was an increasing demand for tradable foodstuffs.

Stockfish was the ideal commodity. Lightweight, durable, and highly nutritious, it could last for years without spoiling and be reconstituted quickly by soaking in water. Demand soared. Bergen, a picturesque seaport founded on the cod trade, became Norway's capital and an important seat in the Hanseatic League, a medieval merchant-trader confederation, with over 2,000 resident members exporting thousands of tons of stockfish each year to Germany, Holland, and England.

While it was the prosperous burghers in town who made most of the profits, the tough peasant fishermen did well too. A man with a boat had his own business, free and clear, with all the lucrative upside that might entail. Reveling in their freedom and spurred by the possibilities of jackpot wealth, these fishermen braved hardships and dangers, sailing north to Lofoten's cod banks each winter as though it were a gold rush—Norway's own annual Klondike.

By the turn of the 20th century, more than 30,000 fishermen were flocking to these islands each winter. Grainy black-and-white photographs show Røst's harbors so jammed with boats that it was possible to walk from one side to the other without getting your feet wet.

"This was Lofoten," Norwegian author Jan Bojer wrote in his 1921 coming-of-age classic, The Last Viking. "A land in the Arctic Ocean that all the boys along the coast dreamed of visiting someday, a land where exploits were performed, fortunes were made, and where fishermen sailed in a race with Death. Through hundreds of years they had migrated thither, and many of them had lost their lives on the sea. A few returned home with well-filled pockets, but the greater number sailed to the end of life in poverty. Yet they went up again and again, year after year, generation after generation. It was their fairy land of fortune. They had to go."

Will young Norwegians keep the stockfish lineage alive?

Times have changed. In a world alive with 21st-century opportunities, young Norwegians no longer daydream about scooping fortunes in cod out of icy midwinter seas. Their aspirations lie elsewhere—in safe, comfortable jobs in distant cities. In recent years they've been leaving their picturesque fishing villages in droves—not just on Røst or Lofoten, but all over Norway.

Even if they wanted to take up fishing, few could afford it. Buying a cod quota—essentially a commercial license to catch cod—can cost as much as half a million dollars. And then you have to buy your boat and equipment, and hire a crew.

It was always a risky proposition, all the more so in an age of changing climates. "Banks are not keen to lend that kind of money to young people just starting out," says Pedersen.

Fishing in Norway is increasingly consolidated in the hands of a few old families or companies with deep pockets, while jobs in the fish factories, or hanging the thousands of cod on wooden frames, are increasingly filled by migrants who flock north, much as in the stories of old.

"The face of the stockfish trade has changed a lot over the past few years," says Olaf Pedersen. "And it will continue to change and evolve. But at the same time, it is still the same business it always was—drying fresh caught cod in the open air."

By midnight the day's catch is hanging on the wooden frames. And under the eerie glow of the Northern Lights begins the age-old curing or fermentation process that will render it into stockfish.

Health Angle
of Stockfish

Stockfish offers several health benefits due to its rich nutritional profile.

- High-Quality Protein: Stockfish is an excellent source of high-quality protein. Unlike some other protein sources, stockfish provides protein without a significant amount of fat.
- Brain Health: Stockfish promotes brain health in multiple ways:
  - ➤ Omega-3 Fatty Acids: It contains omega-3 fatty acids, which help reduce inflammation and improve cognitive function.
  - ➤ B Vitamins: Stockfish is loaded with B vitamins (such as vitamin D, B6, B12, and niacin), essential for maintaining healthy brain function and reducing the risk of cognitive decline.
- Cholesterol Regulation: Consuming stockfish helps maintain healthy cholesterol levels:

- ➤ HDL Cholesterol: It supports HDL cholesterol (the good kind) due to the presence of omega-3 fats.
- ➤ LDL Cholesterol: It helps reduce LDL cholesterol (the bad kind), thus preventing heart diseases associated with high levels of bad cholesterol.
- Nutrient-Rich: Stockfish retains all the nutrients from fresh fish, but in a concentrated form. It is rich in:
  - ➤ Proteins
  - ➤ B Vitamins (including vitamin D, B6, B12, and niacin)
  - ➤ Minerals (such as phosphorus, selenium, and calcium)
- Heart Health: By regulating cholesterol levels, stockfish contributes to overall heart health.
- Immunity: The nutrients in stockfish, including selenium, help defend the body against oxidative stress, thus supporting a robust immune system.
- Eye Health: The presence of essential nutrients like vitamin D and omega-3 fatty acids benefits eye health.

Importance of Culinary Experimentations

As I stated earlier, one of my favorite avocations is "kitchen science experiments," as formally stated in my curriculum vitae. Some professionals love playing golf for recreation and relaxation. Some love playing cards. Some love riding bicycles for fun. Nigerian Yoruba elders love playing the Ayo board game. I love experimenting with new combinations and permutations of ingredients in the kitchen, which may turn out good or bad, and then writing about it as an archival documentation. Experimenting and documenting possess a good linkage. Regardless, I advocate a more adventurous engagement of cooking, beyond conventional recipes and cooking practices. Readers are encouraged to try something new, substitute uncharted ingredients, and experiment with modern healthy choices.

The traditional African recipes that call for the use of palm oil can be revolutionized with olive oil, canola oil, corn oil, peanut oil, or coconut oil. Who knows, a new favorite taste may be discovered. A bit of this, a dash of that, and a sprinkle of spices can lead to new recipe discoveries. Men should, however, be cautious when conducting recipe experiments in the presence of their better halves ---- unless there is a defensible explanation. The following long-ago conversation between my wife and me attests to this suggestion:

Me: "Hymm, this did not turn out as I wished."
My wife: "Wishful thinking does not a recipe make.
            Now, you've ruined a perfectly good fish."
Me: "Well, I learned something new from the
            experiment."
My wife: "What would that happen to be?"
Me: "I learned never to try that again."

In spite of failed experiments, don't be shy. Go ahead and try something new. As it is often said, "Don't quit. Success is failure turned inside out." So, try and try again. Culinary success may be lurking in the next pot of soup. Experimentation is the key.

What would have happened if someone so long ago did not experiment to discover the effect of salt on food flavor or the impact of sugar on the taste of tea? How did we discover the tangs of various spices? In dancing, we can show that the art form of dancing is akin to the special art form of cooking . . . with measured steps serving as ingredients for a visually pleasing rumba. Similarly, writing, which is akin to cooking and dancing, uses carefully selected words to compose sentences, which are choreographed to form articulate paragraphs, which eventually form a prose. Painting follows the same form as a composition of carefully selected shades of color.

I regularly conduct kitchen research. Some turn out great while most turn out to belong on the shelf of lessons learned. I see every failed cooking experiment as a lesson of what not to try in the future. Research and experimentation are essential for creating new and exciting dishes. A family friend provided a supportive and encouraging comment with "I think of you when I am trying new recipes in my kitchen." This is a compliment I am proud of. I am often the bold experimenter while my wife is the developer, who puts finishing touches to new culinary ideas.

Food is a unifying element in family relationships. It brings us together in times of trouble and in times of joy. We celebrate with food. We celebrate food. In a talk about her book, *Recipes for Life,* Dynasty actress Linda Evans says she incorporates memories in her memoir with two of her favorite things --- cooking and eating. It seems to us that she endorses what I now call the new movement of "eatertainment."

Eating is one act that is common to all humans; to all living things for that matter. Even after a period of extended fasting, what follows is an extreme engagement in eating. The act of eating will never go out of vogue. This is why we should celebrate it and write about it.

Of the body, eating provides nourishments that are essential for life, healing, and thriving as a social being. Of the soul, eating offers pleasure that excites the senses that makes a person what he or she is spiritually and socially. While the body represents the engagement of time and space, it is the soul that creates the aura that ties everything together. Essentially, the soul is the atmosphere, spiritual or otherwise, within which the body resides. Of the mind, eating expands the mind both through the anticipatory comfort of the food as well as the gratification of going through the action of consumption. A dull mind can result from not being exposed to a wide variety of tastes.

Efficacy
of Dihydrogen
Monoxide

This is **H_2O** in chemical symbol representation and commonly known to us as water. It is the all-important and much-cherished water in any kitchen. The importance of water fits the theme of this book: Physics in the Nigerian Kitchen. Pure water is odorless, tasteless, and clear. Water is one of nature's most important resources. Our survival depends on drinking water. Water is one of the most essential elements to good health, absorption of food, and digestion. Water also helps to maintain proper muscle tone and helps to convey oxygen and nutrients to cells in the body. Water also rids the body of wastes. For those concerned about their waist lines, it is important to note that water contains no calories. Although water covers more than 70% of the Earth, only 1% of the Earth's water is available as potable water for drinking. So, it is essential to conserve water at every opportunity. Excessive and unnecessary uses of water in the kitchen and bathroom must be avoided.

Key properties of water

- Freezing point of water: 0° C (32° F)
- Boiling point of water: 100° C (212° F).
- Water reaches its maximum density at 4° C (39° F)
- Water expands upon freezing

Water combines with salts to form hydrates and reacts with metal oxides to form acids Occurrence: Water is the only substance that occurs at ordinary temperatures in all three states of matter: solid, liquid, and gas.

Body of Water

"Body of Water" figuratively and biologically refers to the water composition of the human body. The body contains between 55% and 78% depending of body size. Water is a common chemical substance that makes our body healthy. It is composed of hydrogen and oxygen and it is very essential for life. Drinking plenty of water throughout the day helps replenish the water level in the body. It is, thus, essential for body and soul. Lean muscle tissue contains about 99% water by weight. Blood contains almost 50% water, body fat contains 1/2% water and bone has 97% water. Skin also contains much water. On the average, the human body is about 60% water in adult males and 55% in adult females.

Effect of Salt

Apart from flavoring, salt has many other uses. Water and salt are two of the most important essentials in a kitchen. It is interesting to note how they interact to do what we expect of them in terms of our food preparation. The effect of salt on the boiling point of water is particularly of interest, but only for theoretical reasons. For practical kitchen applications, the effect is negligible. But for scientific curiosity, we will examine the effect. Adding salt to water increases the boiling temperature (i.e., boiling point), causing the water to come to a boil more slowly. That is, it requires a higher temperature to boil. This increase in the cooking temperature will cause foods boiled in salt water to cook faster. Pure liquids (e.g., water) will generally have lower boiling points than mixtures (e.g., water and salt). For this reason, adding sugar to water has the same increasing effect on the boiling point as adding salt. If pure water is heated up to a high temperature prior to the addition of the salt, it could cause the entire pot to start boiling spontaneously. This is a result of the grains of salt acting as nucleation sites. This has the effect of making nearly-boiling water actually boil more quickly when salt is added. The tiny amount of salt required to cause a nucleation effect would have no effect on the temperature of the boiling water. In this regard, you can think of the salt as a catalyst, facilitating the change of state of the water from liquid to boiling. Adding salt to water to raise the boiling point for cooking is actually negligible in practice. The amount of salt we normally add to water for typical cooking would have negligible effect on the boiling temperature. To easily remember this relationship, we present the visual plot below, based on a simple lab experiment. For fun experimentation purposes, you can add a few grains of salt to pure water to kick off the boiling process with nucleation; but beyond that, it will not have any noticeable effect on cooking temperature or time.

Facts of Flavor

Temperature and Flavor: Temperature affects flavor. As reported by the November 2012 issue of Reader's Digest, researchers in Belgium found that certain taste bud receptors are most sensitive to food molecules that are at or just above room temperature. So, hot coffee may seem less bitter (i.e., tastes better) because our bitter-detecting taste buds are not as sensitive when coffee is hot. It was also found that odors also influence flavor. Thus, even the most bitter hot coffee may taste delicious because of its pleasant aroma. Coffee at room temperature does not have the same aroma.

Kitchen Management

Of the science and art of homemade Stockfish, what comes after the Stockfish is harvested is the art of cooking.

To cook, you must have a kitchen.

To cook well, your kitchen must be well managed. That's the art of it.

To have a good kitchen product, you must know something about management.

The art of cooking comes glaringly across by the way the kitchen is managed. A poorly managed kitchen will translate to poor gastronomic outputs. The art of Nigerian cooking is, indeed, a special art. Nigerian cooking, like many African-type cooking, involves a lot of undocumented (un-reciped) cooking processes that are honed and handed down through direct observation and domestic apprenticeship. Very much like the African oral history, Nigerian kitchen expertise is handed down through kitchen practice.

Kitchen as My Art Studio

Cooking should be viewed as an avenue for artistic expression. Your kitchen should be viewed as your arts studio. You would not think of an arts studio without basic tools, paints, canvas, and other "ingredients" of beautiful art. Stock your kitchen so that you won't go wanting in the process of creating your work of kitchen art. Unless you have a Nigerian neighbor, you may not be able to go running through the neighborhood in search of who has a box of salt, a packet of sugar, or a sachet of nutmeg at an odd hour of the evening when your guests are about to arrive.

Light up your kitchen

The battle of watts and lumens looms in the kitchen. A kitchen should be well lighted. A question often comes up regarding using a higher wattage bulb to get more light into a room. To clarify, wattage is a measure of energy consumption while lumens represent a measure of light emission. Thus, a bulb that gives off higher lumens is preferred for getting a room better lit. In general, lower-wattage bulbs tend to be less efficient. Thus, if you want more light, it can be achieved with a larger-wattage bulb compared to using multiple smaller-wattage bulbs.

Cooking Process Improvement

The 5s/6s Approach: The concepts expressed above fit the same idea of managing a production environment in industry. Japanese manufacturing operations are well known for their use of specialized management practices to get the most out of their production investments. One of the most popular industrial concepts is the 5s Principle and its extension to 6s. This is a methodology of workplace organization and visual controls. The five "Ss" refer to five Japanese words: seiri, seiton, seiso, seiketsu, and shitsuke.

- Seiri (sort) means to separate needed and unneeded materials and to remove the latter.

- Seiton (stabilize) means to neatly arrange (stabilize or straighten) and identify needed materials for ease of use. This enforces a place for everything and everything in its place. This is a mark of the best cooks.

- Seiso (shine) means to conduct a cleanup campaign. Clean up the workplace and look for ways to keep it clean always.

- Seiketsu (standardize) means to do seiri, seiton, and seiso at frequent intervals and to repeat the 5S procedures.

- Shitsuke (sustain) means to form the habit of always following the first four Ss.

Clearly, every kitchen that is organized according to 5s principle will always produce good results. The 6s Principle adds safety to the 5s approach. Certainly, every kitchen needs to follow safety practices.

- Safety - Eliminate hazards. For example, keep the kitchen safe and operational.

  In some management extension of 5s/6s, the following additional S's are practiced:

- Security – This may relate to security perception and confidence of the worker (e.g., cook).

- Satisfaction – This may relate to job satisfaction and gratification enjoyed by cook in admiring his or her culinary outputs.

Lean Six Sigma in the Kitchen

Imagine a cooking environment that is not consistent. Sometimes, it will produce acceptable results and sometimes it will not. Such a level of inconsistency will not be acceptable in a production environment in industry because many products will end up being rejected. The concept of Lean is to eliminate waste in the production process. Thus, only value-adding functions are allowed. If this concept is implemented in a kitchen, it means that only ingredients that add value (color, taste, aroma, flavor, etc.) are allowed in the cooking process. The concept of

Six Sigma is to reduce variability in the production process using statistical techniques. Six sigma means six standard deviations from a statistical performance average. The six sigma approach allows for no more than 3.4 defects per million parts in manufactured goods or 3.4 mistakes per million activities in a service operation. To appreciate the effect of the six sigma approach, consider a process that is 99% perfect. That process will produce 10,000 defects per million parts. With six sigma, the process will need to be 99.99966% perfect in order to produce only 3.4 defects per million. That means that the area under the normal curve within plus or minus six sigma is 99.9999966% with 0.0000034% defect area. That is, 3.4 defects per million (Note: 3.4/1,000,000 = 0.0000034 = 0.00034%). Thus, Six Sigma is an approach that pushes the limit of perfection to minimize rejected products. Consider a non-six-sigma hamburger cooking process, where five, out of every 100 hamburgers, cooked are rejected for not meeting quality standards. Obviously, such a process will not be good for the company's bottom line (profit). By analogy, that will not be good for the cook's job security and personal satisfaction.

Cooking as a Global Art Form

Cooking is a global art form. We all speak the same language when it comes to the art of loving food, embracing its preparation, and cherishing its consumption. Painting, writing, dancing, and cooking are intertwined as artistic expressions of mood, emotion, ethnicity, and culture all over the world. The lead author is the very embodiment of all the four expressive art form as evidenced by his Ode to cooking, writing, dancing, and painting in the front matter of this book. The foods we love and embrace could be our artistic expression. We are reminded of the literary and artistic linkages of food by the following universal quotes:

"The best poet is the man who delivers our daily bread: the local baker."
- Pablo Neruda

"A bottle of wine contains more philosophy than all the books in the world."
- Louis Pasteur

"A clever cook can make good meat of a whetstone."
- Erasmus

"A first-rate soup is better than a second rate painting."
- Abraham Maslow

"A good cook is like a sorceress who dispenses happiness."
- Elsa Schiaparelli

"A good cook is not necessarily a good woman with an even temper. Some allowance should be made for artistic temperament."
- Marcel Boulestin

"A good dinner is of great importance to good talk. One cannot think well, love well, sleep well, if one has not dined well."
- Virginia Woolf

"A mathematician is a device for turning coffee into theorems."
- Paul Erdos

"A true gastronome should always be ready to eat, just as a soldier should always be ready to fight."
- Charles Pierre Monselet

"All cooks, like all great artists, must have an audience worth cooking for."
- Andre Simon

Culinary Creativity

In the recipe collection in this book, the objective is to be creative and innovative. In practice, there are few recipe rules. Readers can be resourceful in creating their own original, imaginative, and artistic twists to the basics offered in this book. Co-author Deji takes great delight in conducting food science experiments, which he combines with his other varied avocation of dancing, writing, and painting. Cooking, like writing, dancing, and painting, is an art form. He opines:

"You mix carefully selected ingredients to create tasteful dishes and enjoyable meals. In writing, you organize words to compose beautiful sentences, which form enthralling paragraphs, which are concatenated to form a logical flow of reading imagination. In painting, carefully selected colors in varying degrees of intensity and strokes are amalgamated to create gorgeous scenes. In dancing, footwork and carefully placed steps are choreographed to create a beautiful performance. These are all related art forms as I see them. I am fascinated by the dance of the ingredients in the cooking pot."

Culinary creativity and freedom are expressed by M. F. K. Fisher's quote:

"A complete lack of caution is perhaps one of the true signs of a real gourmet: he has no need for it, being filled as he is with a God-given and intelligently self-cultivated sense of gastronomical freedom." - M.F.K. Fisher

Culinary Physics links foods for body and soul and brings ethnic African, particularly Nigerian, traditional recipes to the limelight of international cooking in a formal and recognizable archival form. The important linkage of food and soul is confirmed by Frederick Hackwood:

"A good meal soothes the soul as it regenerates the body. From the abundance of it flows a benign benevolence." - Frederick W. Hackwood

Kitchen Project Management

The tools and techniques of project management are directly applicable to large-scale cooking projects. In this case, we are focusing on large-scale cooking for social events rather than institutional undertakings, like restaurants. A project is conventionally defined as "a unique one-of-a-kind endeavor with a definite beginning and a definite end." Large-scale cooking project do, indeed, have all the makings a conventional project and should be managed accordingly. A project is constituted to achieve one or more of the following three outputs:

1. Produce a physical product
2. Provide a certain service
3. Generate a desired result

A cooking project meets all three of the above output categories. Cooking produces a physical consumable product in terms of menu items. Cooking, particularly through a catering business, provides a service in terms helping to meet the needs of the client to provide food for guests and visitors. Cooking, if done properly, will generate the desired result of quenching hunger while satisfying the palate. Project management is an integral part of human existence and a key factor in achieving operational excellence in technical, professional, and domestic functions. For large-scale cooking projects, the proof of project management pudding is in what comes out of the kitchen.

Seventy-nine percent or more of us are homemakers. Homemakers are not necessarily stay-at-home moms. Even where the percentages inferred from research studies don't correlate, we see more and more, working moms and dads also managing home projects. Kitchen-based projects are particularly common. This makes it imperative to apply project management tools and techniques in the kitchen to save time and improve the cooking process. In order to get the best output of your kitchen, you must manage the kitchen enterprise just as you would manage any personal or professional project.

Based on the definition of homemakers utilized by the U.S. Census Bureau, homemakers are individuals who perform duties or "projects" at home that include home-keeping, cooking, making beds, doing laundry, washing dishes, dusting, assembling products, installing gadgets, managing electronics, monitoring utilities, organizing garages, shoveling snow, decorating, and making household repairs. Homemakers also advise families, provide healthcare, and mete out discipline to kids. These are a whole lot of projects (small or big, easy or difficult, simple or complex) running around the home. Each and every one of them needs help from project management.

In his professional project management textbook, Deji defines project management as "the process of managing, allocating, and timing resources to accomplish objectives in an efficient and expeditious manner."

Steps of Project Management: The objectives of a project may be stated in terms of time (schedule), performance (quality), or cost (budget). Time is often the most critical aspect of managing any project. Time must be managed concurrently with all other important aspects of any project, particularly in an academic setting. Project management covers the basic stages listed below:

1. Initiation
2. Planning
3. Execution
4. Tracking and Control
5. Closure

The stages are often contracted or expanded based on the needs of the specific project. They can also overlap based on prevailing project scenarios. For example, tracking and control often occur concurrently with project execution. Embedded within execution is the function of activity scheduling. If contracted, the list of stages may include only Planning, Organizing, Scheduling, and Control. In this case, closure is seen as a control action. If expanded, the list may include additional explicit stages such as Conceptualization, Scoping, Resource Allocation, and Reporting.

Project Initiation

In the first stage of the project lifecycle, the scope of the project is defined along with the approach to be taken to deliver the desired results. The project manager and project team are appointed based on skills, experience, and relevance. The process of organizing the project is often carried out as a bridge or overlap between initiation and planning. The most common tools used in the initiation stage are Project Charter, Business Plan, Project Framework, Overview, Process Mapping, Business Case Justification, and Milestone Reviews. Project initiation normally takes place after problem identification and project definition.

Project Planning

The second stage of the project lifecycle includes a detailed identification and assignment of tasks making up the project. It should also include a risk analysis and a definition of criteria for the successful completion of each deliverable. During planning, the management process is defined, stakeholders are identified, reporting frequency is established, and communication channels are agreed upon. The most common tools used in the planning stage are Brainstorming, Business Plan, Process Mapping, and Milestones Reviews.

Execution and Control

The most important issue in the execution and control stages of the project lifecycle involves ensuring that tasks are executed expeditiously in accordance with the project plan, which is always subject to re-planning. Tracking is an implicit component and prerequisite for project control. For projects that are organized for producing physical products, a design resulting in a specific set of product requirements is created. The integrity of the product is assured through prototypes, validation, verification, and testing. As the execution phase progresses, groups across the organization become progressively involved in the realization of the project objectives. The most common tools or methodologies used in the execution stage include Risk Analysis, Balance Scorecards, Business Plan Review, and Milestone Assessment.

Project Closure

In the closure stage, the project is phased-out or formally terminated. The closure process is often gradual as the project is weaned of resources and personnel are reallocated to other organizational needs. Acceptance of deliverables is an important part of project closure. The closure phase is characterized by a formal project review covering the following components: a formal acceptance of the final product, Weighted Critical Measurements (matching the initial requirements with the final product delivered), thanking and rewarding the participants, documentation of a list of lessons learned, releasing project resources, doing a formal project closure, and project cleanup. Deji does use project management techniques in his kitchen and home projects.

Kitchen Management Tips

- Plan your cooking project and execute the project according to plan.
- Have contingency plans in case things don't go well.
- Always allow enough time for your cooking project. Quality takes time. A rushed cooking project could become a failed project.
- Manage your kitchen time judiciously. Distractions cost time. Rework also costs time. Preempt accidents and errors that will cost you time in your cooking project.
- For safety reasons, never leave the handle of a pot on the stove hanging over the edge of the stove. Kitchen accidents, even minor ones, cost time in terms of emergency, personal injury, and recovery time.
- Never leave hot food or appliances unattended while cooking. If you are frying, boiling, or broiling food, stay with your *project* in the kitchen. Project monitoring and oversight are essential for any successful project.
- Avoid engaging in a kitchen project if you are impaired due to the influence of medication or drugs.
- Keep anything that can catch on fire at least three feet from the stove, toaster oven, burners, or other heat sources.
- Keep the stovetop, burners, and oven clean before, during, and after each cooking project.
- Do not wear loose fitting clothes when you are cooking. A fire hazard can detract from project success.

- If all the stove burners are not in use when you cook, use the back row burners. This allows for more operational space around the focal point of your project. This also minimizes the risk of a child reaching for any hot stuff on the cooking surface.
- Keep appliance cords coiled, away from the counter edges, and out of reach of children.
- Use oven mitts or pot-holders when carrying hot food.
- Open hot containers from the microwave slowly and away from your face.
- Never use a wet oven mitt, as it presents a scalding risk if the moisture in the mitt is heated.
- Never hold a child while cooking, carrying or drinking hot foods or liquids. Multi-tasking with kid care is a no-no in the kitchen zone.

Appendix: Useful Conversion Factors

Mathematical conversions from one space, time, and dimension into another are essential for many of the technological advancements that we enjoy today, from transportation and recreation to exploration and to kitchen experiments too. This section presents selected useful conversion factors. Conversions of distance, weight, volume, and so on affect everything we do at home, at work, in commerce, and at leisure.

Kilometer-Mile Conversions			
Kilometers to	Miles	Miles to	Kilometers
1	0.6	1	1.6
5	3.1	5	8.05
10	6.2	10	16.0
20	12.4	20	32.1
30	18.6	30	48.2
40	24.8	40	64.3
50	31.1	50	80.5
60	37.3	60	96.6
70	43.5	70	112.7

80	49.7	80	128.7
90	55.9	90	144.8
100	62.1	100	160.9
500	310.7	500	804.7
1,000	621.4	1,000	1609.3

Metric Tables

Capacity		Area	
10 milliliters	= 1 centiliter	100 sq. millimeters	= 1 sq. centimeter
10 centiliters	= 1 deciliter	100 sq. centimeters	= 1 sq. decimeter
10 deciliters	= 1 liter	100 sq. decimeters	= 1 sq. meter (centare)
10 liters	= 1 dekaliter	100 sq. meters	= 1 are
10 dekaliters	= 1 hectoliter	10,000 sq. meters	= 1 hectare
1,000 liters	= 1 kiloliter (stere)	100 hectares	= 1 sq. kilometer
LENGTH		WEIGHT	
10 millimeters	= centimeter (cm)	10 milligrams	= 1 centigram
10 centimeters	= 1 decimeter	10 centigrams	= 1 decigram
10 decimeters	= 1 meter (m)	10 decigrams	= 1 gram
10 meters	= 1 dekameter	1,000 grams	= 1 kilogram (kilo)
100 meters	= 1 hectometer	100 kilograms	= 1 quintal
1,000 meters	= 1 kilometer	1,000 kilograms	= 1 metric ton

Metric Equivalent Of U.S. Weights And Measures

DRY MEASURE		LONG MEASURE	
1 Pint	= .550599 liter	1 inch	= 2.54 centimeters
1 quart	= 1.101197 liters	1 yard	= .914401 meter
1 peck	= 8.80958 liters	1 mile	= 1.609347 kilometers
1 bushed	= .35238 hectoliter		

LIQUID MEASURE		SQUARE MEASURE	
1 Pint	= .473167 liter	1 sq. inch	6.4516 sq.
1 quart	= .946332 liter	1 sq. foot	centimeters
1 gallon	= 3.785329 liters	1 sq. yard	9.29034 sq.
		1 acre	decimeters
		1 sq. mile	.836131 sq. meter
		1 sq. mile	.40469 hectares
			2.59 sq.
			kilometers
			259 hectares
AVOIRDUPOIS MEASURE		CUBIC MEASURE	
1 ounce	= 28.349527 grams	1 cu. Inch	= 16.3872 cu.
1 pound	= .453592	1 cu. Foot	Centimeters
1 short ton	kilograms	1 cu. yard	= .028317 cu. Meter
1 long ton	= .90718486		= .76456 cu meter
	metric ton		
	= 1.01604704		
	metric tons		

Useful Mathematical Relationships

$$\sin \theta = \frac{b}{c} \qquad \csc \theta = \frac{c}{b}$$

$$\sin \theta = \frac{a}{c} \qquad \sec \theta = \frac{c}{a}$$

$$\tan \theta = \frac{b}{a} \qquad \cot \theta = \frac{a}{b}$$

1 radian	$= 57.3°$
1 inch	$= 2.54$ cm
1 gallon	$= 231$ in^3
1 kilogram	$= 2.205$ lb
1 newton	$= 1$ kg $\bullet$ m/s^2
1 joule	$= 1$ N $\bullet$ m
1 watt	$= 1$ J/s
1 pascal	$= 1$ N/m^2
1 BTU	$= 778$ ft-lb
	$= 252$ cal
	$= 1,054.8$ J
1 horsepower	$= 745.7$ W
1 atmosphere	$= 14.7$ lb/in^2
	$= 1.01 \bullet 10^5$ N/m^2

Mathematical Constants

Speed of light	$2.997,925 \times 10^{10}$ cm/sec
	983.6×10^{6} ft/sec
	186,284 miles/sec
Velocity of sound	340.3 meters/sec
	1116 ft/sec
Gravity	9.80665 m/sec square
(acceleration)	32.174 ft/sec square
	386.089 inches/sec square

Area Relationships

Multiply	by	to obtain
acres	43,560	sq feet
	4,047	sq meters
	4,840	sq yards
	0.405	hectare
sq cm	0.155	sq inches
sq feet	144	sq inches
	0.09290	sq meters
	0.1111	sq yards
sq inches	645.16	sq millimeters
sq kilometers	0.3861	sq miles
sq meters	10.764	sq feet
	1.196	sq yards
sq miles	640	acres
	2.590	sq kilometers

Volume Relationships

Multiply	by	to obtain
acre-foot	1233.5	cubic meters
cubic cm	0.06102	cubic inches
cubic feet	1728	cubic inches
	7.480	gallons (US)
	0.02832	cubic meters
	0.03704	cubic yards
liter	1.057	liquid quarts
	0.908	dry quarts
	61.024	cubic inches
gallons (US)	231	cubic inches
	3.7854	liters
	4	quarts
	0.833	British gallons
	128	U.S. fluid ounces
quarts (US)	0.9463	liters

Energy And Heat Power Relationships

Multiply	by	to obtain
BTU	1055.9	joules
	0.2520	kg-calories
watt-hour	3600	joules
	3.409	BTU
HP (electric)	746	watts
BTU/second	1055.9	watts
watt-second	1.00	joules

Mass Relationships

Multiply	by	to obtain
carat	0.200	cubic grams
grams	0.03527	ounces
kilograms	2.2046	pounds
ounces	28.350	grams
pound	16	ounces
	453.6	grams
stone (UK)	6.35	kilograms
	14	pounds
ton (net)	907.2	kilograms
	2000	pounds
	0.893	gross ton
	0.907	metric ton
ton (gross)	2240	pounds
	1.12	net tons
	1.016	metric tons
tonne (metric)	2,204.623	pounds
	0.984	gross pound
	1000	kilograms

Temperature Relationships

Conversion formulas

Celsius to Kelvin	$K = C + 273.15$
Celsius to Fahrenheit	$F = (9/5)C + 32$
Fahrenheit to Celsius	$C = (5/9)(F - 32)$
Fahrenheit to Kelvin	$K = (5/9)(F + 459.67)$
Fahrenheit to Rankin	$R = F + 459.67$
Rankin to Kelvin	$K = (5/9)R$

Velocity Relationships

Multiply	by	to obtain
feet/minute	5.080	mm/second
feet/second	0.3048	meters/second
inches/second	0.0254	meters/second
km/hour	0.6214	miles/hour
meters/second	3.2808	feet/second
	2.237	miles/hour
miles/hour	88.0	feet/minute
	0.44704	meters/second
	1.6093	km/hour
	0.8684	knots
knot	1.151	miles/hour

Pressure Relationships

Multiply	by	to obtain
atmospheres	1.01325	bars
	33.90	feet of water
	29.92	inches of mercury
	760.0	mm of mercury
bar	75.01	cm of mercury
	14.50	pounds/sq inch
dyne/sq cm	0.1	N/sq meter
newtons/sq cm	1.450	pounds/sq inch
pounds/sq inch	0.06805	atmospheres
	2.036	inches of mercury
	27.708	inches of water
	68.948	millibars
	51.72	mm of mercury

Distance Relationships

Multiply	by	to obtain
angstrom	10^{-10}	meters
feet	0.30480	meters
	12	inches
inches	25.40	millimeters
	0.02540	meters
	0.08333	feet
kilometers	3280.8	feet
	0.6214	miles
	1094	yards
meters	39.370	inches
	3.2808	feet
	1.094	yards
miles	5280	feet
	1.6093	kilometers
	0.8694	nautical miles
millimeters	0.03937	inches
nautical miles	6076	feet
	1.852	kilometers
yards	0.9144	meters
	3	feet
	36	inches

Common Mathematical Notations

UNITS OF MEAS.	ABBREV.	RELATION	UNITS OF MEAS.	ABBREV.	RELATION
meter	m	length	degree Celsius	°C	temperature
hectare	ha	area	Kelvin	K	thermodynamic temp.
tonne	t	mass	pascal	Pa	pressure, stress
kilogram	kg	mass	joule	J	energy, work
nautical mile	M	distance (navigation)	Newton	N	force
knot	kn	speed (navigation)	watt	W	power, radiant flux
liter	L	volume or capacity	ampere	A	electric current
second	s	time	volt	V	electric potential
hertz	Hz	frequency	ohm	Ω	electric resistance
candela	cd	luminous intensity	coulomb	C	electric charge

Kitchen Measurements

A pinch .... 1/8 tsp. or less

3 tsp. .... 1 tbsp.

2 tbsp. .... 1/8 c.

4 tbsp. .... 1/4 c.

16 tbsp. .... 1 c.

5 tbsp. + 1 tsp. .... 1/3 c.

4 oz. .... 1/2 c.

8oz. .... 1 c.

16 oz. .... 1 lbs.

1 oz. .... 2 tbsp. fat or liquid

1 c. of liquid .... 1/2 pt.

2 c. .... 1 pt.

2 pt. .... 1 qt.

4 c. of liquid .... 1 qt.

4 qts. .... 1 gallon

8 qts. .... 1 peck (such as apples, pears, etc.)

1 jigger .... 1 ½ fl.oz.

1 jigger .... 3 tbsp.

Printed in the United States
by Baker & Taylor Publisher Services